Contents

A Harcourt Achieve Imprint

www.Steck-Vaughn.com
1-800-531-5015

What if you could shrink to the size of a grain of sand? People would need a microscope to see you! You could travel anywhere—even into someone's bloodstream! I'm Marcella, Science Officer for the Gene Team.

These interesting facts will help us heal our patient.

Big Ideas

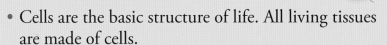

- Cells are the basic structure of life. All living tissues are made of cells.

- Cells reproduce in a process known as cell division.

- Genes are the blueprint for all living things. They determine millions of details, such as height and eye color. Healthy genes can help repair some kinds of damaged cells.

- Arteries are blood vessels that carry blood away from the heart. Veins carry blood back to the heart. Capillaries are the smallest blood vessels. They pass food and oxygen to the tissues in the body.

- Blood pressure is the force of the blood passing through the arteries, veins, and the heart.

Our last mission was exciting. Everything was smooth sailing for a while. Then, our patient's body mistook our ship for a virus! We were attacked by our own patient!

Make sure you know these words. They'll help you follow our medical adventure.

Vocabulary

analyze to look closely at the facts in order to understand them
*Our mechanic used a computer to **analyze** the engine.*

cell a very small unit of life; all living things are made of cells
*Muscle tissues can be made from several kinds of **cells**.*

distinguish to tell the difference between one thing and another
*Some people can't **distinguish** between the colors purple and indigo.*

genetic having to do with genes, the units that determine how things will grow
*That boy's **genetics** should make him very tall when he grows up.*

immune protected against a disease
*Pets are given shots to make them **immune** to rabies.*

Characters

Claude,
Captain of the Gene Team

Suki,
Navigation Officer

Marcella,
Science Officer

Jacob,
Security Officer

Doctor Shrinkenstein,
Head of Mission Control

5

6

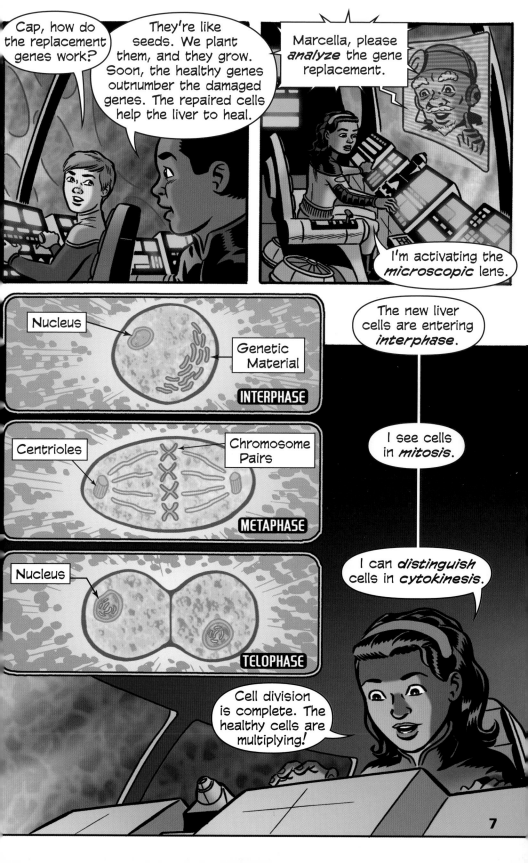

8

13

14

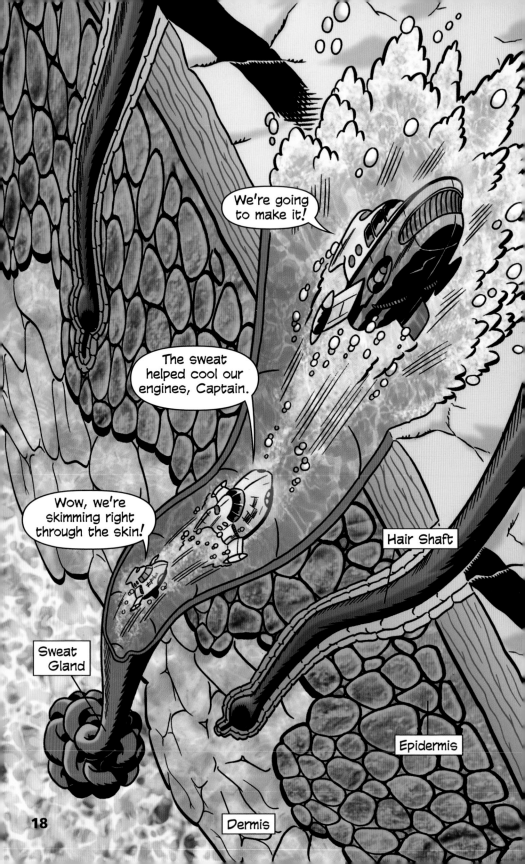

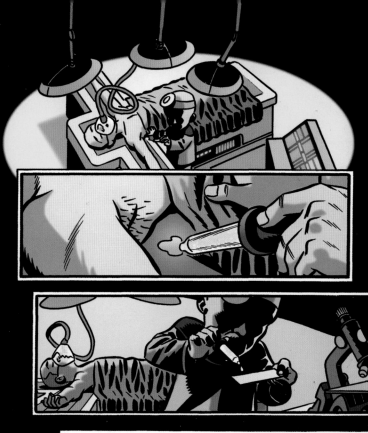

Wrap Up

That was quite an adventure! We replaced the damaged genes—and we also made it out alive! Here are some notes I took during our trip.

- In gene replacement therapy, healthy genes replace damaged genes. The healthy cells reproduce in a process known as cell division.

- The human body has an immune system. Its white blood cells fight infections or invaders in the blood system.

- The human heart is strong enough to pump blood through thousands of miles of veins and arteries. The walls of arteries may expand and contract to help push blood along. You can feel this throbbing as your pulse.

To discover more fun things about genes and the human body, be sure to check out *The Cloning Controversy*.

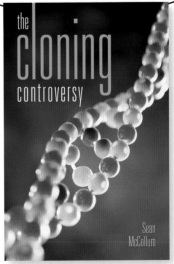

Glossary

analyze (*verb*) to look closely at the facts in order to understand them

capillary (*noun*) a very narrow blood vessel that feeds oxygen to cells

cell (*noun*) a very small unit of life; all living things are made of cells

cytokinesis (*noun*) the division of a cell's cytoplasm during mitosis

distinguish (*verb*) to tell the difference between one thing and another

fever (*noun*) a body temperature that is higher than normal, often to fight infection or illness

genetic (*adjective*) having to do with genes, the units that determine how things will grow

immune (*adjective*) protected against a disease

immunosuppressive (*adjective*) used to slow the immune system, often to prevent the body from rejecting a transplanted organ

initiate (*verb*) to start

interphase (*noun*) the time when a cell is not dividing

lymphatic (*adjective*) having to do with the system of vessels that transport fluids and proteins to the bloodstream

microscopic (*adjective*) so small that it can only be seen with a microscope

mitosis (*noun*) the process by which a cell divides into two cells

plaque (*noun*) a deposit of fatty material

propel (*verb*) to move forward or onward

theory (*noun*) an idea or set of ideas that tries to explain something

utilize (*verb*) to use in an effective and useful way

vessel (*noun*) a tube or canal that carries blood or other fluids

Idioms

get it (*page 10*) understand
Now that I get it, math is more fun.

smooth sailing (*page 3*) going well; proceeding without a problem
It was smooth sailing during my speech—until I dropped my notes!